TURNING POINTS IN HISTORY

The Long March

The Making of Communist China

TONY ALLAN

Heinemann
LIBRARY

www.heinemann.co.uk
Visit our website to find out more information about Heinemann Library books.

To order:

 Phone 44 (0) 1865 888066

Send a fax to 44 (0) 1865 314091

Visit the Heinemann Bookshop at www.heinemann.co.uk to browse our catalogue and order online.

First published in Great Britain by Heinemann Library, Halley Court, Jordan Hill, Oxford OX2 8EJ, a division of Reed Educational and Professional Publishing Ltd. Heinemann is a registered trademark of Reed Educational & Professional Publishing Limited.

OXFORD MELBOURNE AUCKLAND JOHANNESBURG BLANTYRE
GABORONE IBADAN PORTSMOUTH NH (USA) CHICAGO

© Reed Educational and Professional Publishing Ltd 2001
The moral right of the proprietor has been asserted.

Produced for Heinemann Library by Discovery Books Limited
Designed by Ian Winton
Illustrations by Stefan Chabluk
Printed in Hong Kong

05 04 03 02 01
10 9 8 7 6 5 4 3 2 1

ISBN 0 431 06907 7

British Library Cataloguing in Publication Data

Allan, Tony, 1946–
    The long march : the making of communist China. - (Turning points in history)
    1. China - History - 1949 - Juvenile literature
    2. China - Politics and government - 1949 - Juvenile literature
    I. Title
    951'.05

Acknowledgements
The Publishers would like to thank the following for permission to reproduce photographs:
Camera Press, pp. 15, 24, 26; *Corbis (Hulton Deutsch Collection)* p. 11; *Corbis (Lowell Georgia)* p. 18; *Corbis (Brian Vikander)* pp. 5 and front cover (bottom); *Hulton Deutsch Collection*, p. 23; *Hulton Getty*, pp. 6, 8, 10, 13, 17, 20, 21; *Peter Newark's Historical Pictures*, pp. 4 and front cover (top), 9, 12, 14, 19, 27; *Popperfoto*, pp. 7, 22, 25, 28, 29.

Cover photographs reproduced with permission of Corbis and Peter Newark's Historical Pictures.

Every effort has been made to contact copyright holders of any material reproduced in this book. Any omissions will be rectified in subsequent printings if notice is given to the Publisher.

Any words appearing in the text in bold, **like this**, are explained in the Glossary.

Contents

An epic of endurance

In the latter stages of the Long March, Red Army soldiers struggle up a 4000-metre high pass in the Snowy Mountains. The mountain crossing was a particular ordeal for the troops, who were mostly southerners unused to ice and snow and whose quilted cotton tunics could not keep out the cold.

Crossing the Dadu River

The soldiers were already exhausted, but they were tough and battle-hardened. They were the Red Army, Chinese **Communists**, heading north after eight years of **civil war** to escape destruction by their **Nationalist** enemies. They had already travelled some 7000 kilometres (4400 miles) from their original base in southern China, but they still had far to go. Now the success of the entire enterprise hung on finding a crossing over the mighty Dadu River.

There were only two bridges they could take across the river, and both were held by the enemy. The one they chose to attack was the Luding suspension bridge, an ancient structure built of massive iron chains. To take its Nationalist defenders by surprise, a regiment struck out through the mountains, covering 150 kilometres (95 miles) in two days.

The battle for the bridge

When they arrived, they found that the planking had been removed from their end of the bridge. So an assault force of 22 men took to the chains, swaying above the river. Some were shot, but most struggled on to reach the planks - only to find that they had been doused in kerosene. When the defenders set the bridge alight, the Red Army soldiers ran on through the flames, firing machine guns as they went. More troops followed, and within two hours the Red Army had won a vital bridgehead over the river.

A fighting retreat

The capture of the Luding bridge became the most famous exploit in what was to go down in history as the Long March. Lasting a year in all, the march was a fighting retreat by the Red Army that turned into a daily struggle for survival. By winning through to their goal in northern China, the Communist forces lived to fight on - and to reap their reward fourteen years later, when they finally won control of the whole country.

A detail from the Monument to the Heroes of the People, in China's capital of Beijing. It honours the Red Army soldiers who made the Long March in 1934-35. When the Communists came to power in 1949, they celebrated it as the crucial test that had forged their success and changed the fate of the nation.

VICTORY FROM DEFEAT

The Communist leader Mao Zedong (also spelt Mao Tse-tung) summed up the Long March: *'For twelve months we were under daily **reconnaissance** and bombing from the air. We were encircled, pursued, obstructed and intercepted on the ground by a force of several hundred thousand men. We encountered untold difficulties and obstacles on the way, but by keeping our two feet going we swept across a distance of more than 10,000 kilometres (6000 miles)…Has there ever been a long march like ours?'*

China in disarray

An ancient civilization

China traces its history in an unbroken line back to 1766 BCE – a thousand years before the beginning of Roman civilization. Many centuries before the birth of Christ it was producing great poets and philosophers. In later eras it pioneered major technological advances long before they were known anywhere else, among them paper, printing, gunpowder and the magnetic compass.

Boatmen ply their trade outside the walls of old Beijing in this 19th-century engraving. By the 1830s the Chinese capital, like the nation itself, was in decline, though it still preserved the relics of its former grandeur.

From 221 BCE on, the nation was united under the rule of a single emperor, and for the most part imperial government brought China unmatched levels of peace and stability. Yet by the middle of the 19th century, things were going badly wrong. The nation had become backward looking, fearful of change. Convinced its own ways were best, it had cut itself off from the rest of the world, looking on foreigners as barbarians from whom it had nothing to learn. Imperial government protected the interests of a few wealthy landowners; the **illiterate** peasants who made up the bulk of the population barely scraped a living.

The West catches up

Meanwhile the rest of the world had been catching up. Thanks to advances made possible by the scientific revolution of the 17th century, the West had overtaken China economically and technologically. The nation that had once led the way now lagged behind the developing western world.

China's backwardness was cruelly highlighted in a series of disastrous wars. In 1842 the British, defending what they considered their free-trade right to import opium into the country, defeated the Chinese emperor's forces and annexed Hong Kong. Then the French seized Indo-China (today's Vietnam), Laos and Kampuchea, while the Russians took parts of Chinese Turkestan. In 1895, the Japanese captured the island of Formosa (now called Taiwan) and forced China to give up her long-standing influence over Korea. At home discontent flared in two great rebellions, the Taiping rising of the 1850s and 1860s and the Boxer revolt in 1900. Both were put down only with the help of foreign troops. National **morale** plummeted.

A low ebb

Meanwhile, in the Chinese capital of Beijing, an imperial **concubine** seized power in a palace coup to rule as the **Dowager** Empress Ci Xi. Crushing all attempts at reform, she only held on to power with the tacit support of the very foreign powers that had done so much to weaken China. The once great nation's fortunes were at a low ebb.

Addicts in a 19th-century opium den. The drug played a central role in China's collapse. Known as 'foreign mud', by the 1830s as many as 12 million people were addicted to it. When reformers tried to ban its use, the British, who were the main importers, went to war to defend their merchants' trading rights. The Chinese were defeated, and the deadly traffic continued.

Revolution and after

Pu-Yi, China's last emperor, poses in the imperial robes. Just five years old when he lost the throne, he was allowed to remain for the next 12 years in the palace from which his ancestors had ruled the nation.

Imperial rule ends

When Ci Xi died in 1908, leaving the nation in the hands of a new emperor, Pu-Yi, who was just two years old, most Chinese accepted the need for reform. The main spokesman for radical change was Sun Zhongshan (also spelt Sun Yat-sen), a doctor who had spent much of his life abroad putting forward the case for revolution in China. He got his chance in 1911, when province after province rose in revolt againsts the court-appointed officials who were in effect ruling the country. In February 1912, the infant emperor officially **abdicated** in favour of a new, **constitutional** republic. In so doing, he brought more than 2000 years of imperial rule in China to an end.

But it was one thing to bring the old order down and quite another to set up a new one in its place. For all its faults, the imperial system had provided a focus for people's loyalties; with the emperor gone, there was no-one to hold the nation together. Within weeks the country fell into the hands of Yuan Shikai, the former war minister, who tried unsuccessfully to set himself up as a new emperor. After his death in 1916, China simply fell apart.

The warlord era

The next ten years of China's history are known as the **warlord** era. Power in the country's regions fell into the hands of whoever had the strength to seize it. Usually that meant commanders in the Republican army, whose authority rested on force alone. To keep their position, they relied on the backing of soldiers they could barely afford to pay. By the end of the era, it was reckoned that China had 84 separate armies with over 2 million soldiers between them, and that the cost of supporting them all would have added up to more than twice the national budget. In practice many simply went unpaid, living off the countryside as bandits.

In its long imperial history, China had known such periods of **anarchy** before. Now the nation waited helplessly; one system of government had gone, but as yet there was nothing to replace it.

Delegates of the **Guomindang** (also spelt Kuomintang) or **Nationalist** party founded by Sun Zhongshan gather in Beijing. The Nationalists were the driving force behind the revolution that swept away imperial rule in 1912.

A TIME OF HORRORS

In the chaos of the warlord years, armed gangs roamed the land. A 1929 report described how they treated civilians in one part of central China: *'When they capture a person for ransom, they first pierce his legs with iron wire and bind them together as fish are hung on a string… The captives are **interrogated** and cut with sickles to make them disclose hidden property.'*

Nationalists and Communists

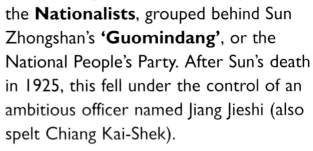

The rise of Jiang Jieshi

In the chaos engulfing China, two movements vied to bring the nation back together. First and biggest were the **Nationalists**, grouped behind Sun Zhongshan's **'Guomindang'**, or the National People's Party. After Sun's death in 1925, this fell under the control of an ambitious officer named Jiang Jieshi (also spelt Chiang Kai-Shek).

The other was the **Communist** Party. Taking their inspiration from the Russian Revolution of 1917, Chinese Communists looked for advice and funding to Moscow, where many of them went for political and military training. There they learned the official **Marxist** line, that revolution would be brought about by industrial workers in the cities, though this seemed unlikely in China, which had little industry but many millions of hungry peasants.

Sun Zhongshan's successor as leader of the Nationalist movement was Jiang Jieshi, shown here in hat and calf-length cloak. Jiang first took on the **warlords** who had divided up China between them. Then he launched a bitter civil war against the Communists with whom he had earlier been allied.

A CLASH OF IDEAS

Although they fought a bitter 22-year **civil war**, Nationalists and Communists shared some common goals. Both wanted to see a strong, prosperous China. The Nationalists sought to achieve that aim through Western-style **private enterprise**. The Communists wanted to transform society from the bottom up. Firstly by giving land to the peasants, then developing industry through state ownership, with the ruling Communist Party, rather than private individuals, taking the decisions and sharing out the rewards.

The Northern Expedition

At first, with Moscow's encouragement, Nationalists and Communists worked together to reunite the nation and defeat the warlords. Prospects looked bright in 1926 when Jiang launched his Northern Expedition, driving towards the old imperial capital of Beijing from his base in southern China. But secretly Jiang had already decided to break with his Communist allies. He did so in dramatic fashion the following year, joining with gangsters to launch a surprise attack on striking workers in the city of Shanghai. In the fighting, thousands of people, including several Communist leaders, were killed.

Civil war breaks out

Following the Shanghai Purge, Nationalists and Communists were deadly enemies, locked in a savage civil war. At first Jiang's forces had the upper hand. Driven out of the cities, the Communists regrouped in half-a-dozen scattered base areas they called '**soviets**'. In the prevailing **anarchy**, it was easy to dismiss them as mere bandits, little different from the other groups of lawless soldiers living off the land all over China. In fact, though, they were tightly disciplined. Toughened by their setbacks, they were biding their time.

A suspected Communist agitator is stopped and searched by military police during the Shanghai Purge of 1927, organized by Jiang Jieshi after pro-Communist trade unions tried to seize control of the city. About 5000 Communists and their supporters were killed.

The loss of Manchuria

The Japanese enter the picture

As if China's internal troubles were not enough, its weakness also attracted outside aggressors. The Japanese had modernized their society in the late 19th century in a way that the Chinese had failed to do. Now their military leaders looked hungrily at China's vast expanses, seeing in them a chance to solve their own overpopulation problem. Japan consisted of a series of mountainous islands with only narrow lowland coastal regions available for people to live in.

They had already defeated China before in 1895, going on to take over the supposedly independent kingdom of Korea. Then, after World War I, in which they backed the USA and Britain, the Japanese were rewarded with bases taken away from defeated Germany in China's northern province of Manchuria.

A recruiting poster for the Japanese army's tank corps demonstrates the militarist spirit that swept Japan in the 1930s.

Crisis in Manchuria

By the start of the 1930s, the Japanese military were eager for more. In 1931 they **sabotaged** a railway line provoking a crisis in Manchuria, which they used as an excuse to take over the whole province. The civilian government in Tokyo went along with them, declaring Manchuria the so-called 'independent' state of Manchukuo and setting up Pu-Yi, the boy emperor the Chinese had got rid of in 1912, as its **puppet ruler**. In 1933 Japanese forces went on to seize the neighbouring Chinese province of Jehol.

The Japanese seizure of Manchuria was not just a blow to Chinese prestige, it was an economic disaster as well. The region was one of the country's richest. With its capture, China lost more than 40 per cent of her railways, most of her coal and iron deposits and almost half her export trade, as well as about a fifth of her territory.

All Chinese were shocked by this blatant assault on their homeland, but in their divided state there was little they could do about it. Realizing that his forces were too weak to defeat the invaders, Jiang Jieshi decided to make the best of a bad job by concentrating on beating the **Communists**. *'The Japanese are a disease of the skin,'* he later declared; *'the Communists are a disease of the heart.'*

Jiang's decision came at a price. Patriotic opinion was deeply offended by his failure to confront the Japanese. In the long run his half-heartedness in opposing them was to prove a costly error.

THE LAST EMPEROR

In 1932 Pu-Yi, last emperor of China, was plucked from obscurity by the Japanese invaders in northern China to be puppet ruler of their newly created state of Manchukuo. Following Japan's defeat in World War II, he lost a second throne. Imprisoned by the Communists in 1949, he was released ten years later and ended his life quietly, working as a gardener in the Beijing botanical gardens.

Japanese troops advance during their 1931 takeover of the Chinese province of Manchuria.

The Long March begins

Communist stronghold in Jiangxi

The Japanese **incursion** came at a time when Jiang Jieshi's **Nationalists** were extending their grip. Since the success of the Northern Expedition, his **Guomindang** party had established itself as the accepted government of the nation, though it had firm control only in the south-east. Elsewhere the **warlords** remained in charge, only paying lip-service to Jiang as their leader.

To most outsiders at the time, the **Communists** looked like a spent force. But they had set up one sizeable **enclave** in Jiangxi province on the borders of Jiang's south-eastern stronghold. There they ruled a region of several million people, gaining the support of the peasants by introducing reforms like the redistribution of land. Sharing out the land more equally was popular because it gave the peasants a better chance of providing for themselves.

Mao Zedong, the future leader of the Chinese Communists, addresses an audience of peasant representatives at a conference in 1933. The 40-year-old revolutionary had risen to prominence by setting up China's largest Communist base in Jiangxi province in the early 1930s.

A wall of fire

Jiang launched four successive offensives against the Communists in the Jiangxi **soviet**, all without success. Eventually, in 1934, he threw all his resources into the so-called Fifth **Annihilation** Campaign, encircling the soviet behind a 'fiery wall' of **scorched earth** and burned villages. The plan was to starve the rebels out.

Through the spring and summer of 1934, the Communists' position grew more critical. Eventually the leadership came to a desperate decision: to burst through the ring, abandoning their most important base to the enemy.

Into the unknown

The plan required absolute secrecy to have any chance of success. In all some 85,000 fighting men were **mobilized**, with no notion of where they were going. When the first units moved out on the night of 16 October, they could hardly have guessed that they were setting out on an epic trek that would take them over 10,000 kilometres (6000 miles) of some of the roughest terrain in China.

Shown here on horseback on the Long March, Zhou Enlai (also spelt Chou Enlai) was to become Mao's right-hand man. After the Communist takeover of China in 1949, Zhou went on to serve as the country's premier and foreign minister, becoming the leading voice for moderation in the government.

North to Shaanzi

Breaking free

The Red Army's sudden departure took the **Nationalist** enemy by surprise, and the **Communist** soldiers had relatively little trouble breaking through the encircling Nationalist forces. At first they headed west, hoping to join up with another **soviet** in neighbouring Hunan province. But Jiang's forces shadowed them all the way, inflicting heavy casualties and preventing them from reaching their destination.

THE GOOD TIMES

One veteran of the march later recalled: *'Night marching is wonderful if there is a moon and a gentle wind blowing… If it was a dark night and the enemy was far away, we would make torches from pine branches or frayed bamboo, and then it was truly beautiful. At the foot of a mountain, we could look up and see a long column of lights coiling like a fiery dragon up the hillside.'*

China during the Long March.

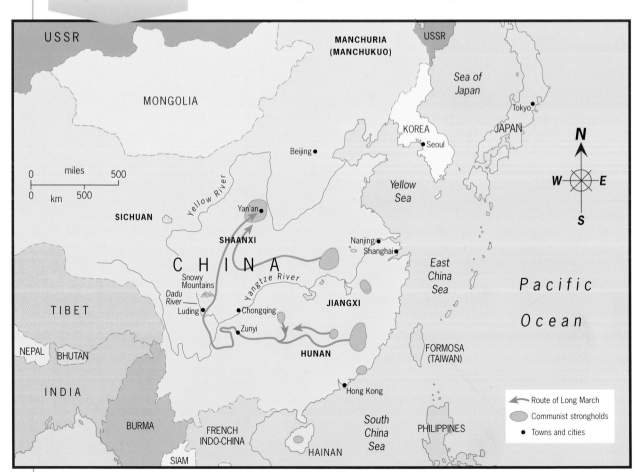

Mao to the fore

It was at this critical point that Mao Zedong came to the fore. The son of wealthy peasants, he had set up the Jiangxi base only to be side-lined by people appointed by Moscow who distrusted his belief in a peasant-based revolution. Now, at a conference of the Communist leadership in January 1935 in the provincial town of Zunyi, Mao's supporters brushed the Moscow faction aside. From that time on Mao was to be the guiding force of Chinese Communism – a position he would hold until his death 41 years later.

Mao led the Red Army west and then north through China's mountainous backbone – punishing country where enemy troops would have difficulty massing in force. The route he chose exposed the marchers to many hardships. Some froze to death crossing the Snowy Mountains; others were lost in the trackless bogs of the grasslands, where men sometimes had to sleep back to back on clumps of grass because there was not enough dry land to lie down.

Home at last

In October 1935, the tired remnants of the Red Army finally reached Shaanxi province, where they joined up with other Communist forces established there since 1930. The 85,000 who had set out had shrunk through death and **desertion** to 20,000, and they had left most of their equipment behind on the way. But they were undefeated and their **morale** was high. The Long March had let them live to fight another day.

Young volunteers line up to join the Long March towards journey's end. While the vast bulk of those who made the journey were men, women were also welcome among the marchers, and a handful travelled the full 10,000 kilometres.

Mao's social experiment

An unpromising beginning

At the Long March's end, Mao and his comrades found themselves in control of a region of north-eastern China so remote that only a single motor road connected it to the rest of the country. Its half a million inhabitants were **illiterate** peasants barely producing enough food to feed themselves; there had been a terrible famine just six years earlier. Now they were to be the target first of a **Nationalist** blockade and later of Japanese bombing. For protection from air attack, Mao's soldiers took to living in caves hollowed out of the soft rock of the local hills.

Today, Yan'an is a modern provincial centre, but when Mao Zedong made it his headquarters in 1936 it was only connected to the rest of China by a single motor road. Its remoteness made it a safe haven for the Communists, who used it as their capital for the next ten years.

Soldiers and peasants

At first sight it seemed unpromising territory for a social experiment, but Mao, as chairman of the Shaanxi **soviet**, set about putting his ideas for a revolutionary society into practice. **Self-sufficiency** was vital, so Red Army soldiers went to classes in sewing and weaving to learn how to make their own clothes. They worked in the fields alongside the peasants; later the **Communists** would claim that the harvest doubled under their care. Even so, there was rarely enough food, and a typical day's diet consisted only of a few cups of barley or millet and a little cabbage.

The other main strand of Mao's programme was education. Soldiers and peasants alike learned to read and write, and there were campaigns aimed at getting rid of superstition and improving **hygiene**. A medical school and technical institutes were set up – even

an academy of arts. Just as important to Mao was political **indoctrination**. Newspapers preached the Communist line, and the Kangda military and political institute which he established attracted radical students from all over China. Meanwhile he grouped around himself a core of key supporters, most of them veterans of the march, who would in later years provide the leadership of the nation.

Telling the world

An American journalist called Edgar Snow found his way to Mao's headquarters in the town of Yan'an and wrote a book about what he saw there. Called *Red Star over China*, it was an international bestseller. Mao's name became known around the world. The Communists were no longer the anonymous 'red bandits' described in **Guomindang propaganda**; they were increasingly seen as serious contenders for power, with their own radical solutions for the nation's overwhelming problems.

Shown here talking to peasants in 1939, Mao's political strategy was based on organizing revolt in the countryside rather than the cities. The tactic worked well, as China had little heavy industry but many millions of poor and hungry land-workers who provided the Red Army with a steady flow of new recruits.

The struggle for China

The Japanese strike south

At first Jiang Jieshi was as eager to destroy the new **Communist** base in Shaanxi as he had been to demolish the Jiangxi **soviet**. But he had misjudged the mood of the nation, which was more concerned with the Japanese threat. On a trip north he was seized by a Manchurian **warlord**, who agreed to release him only in exchange for a pledge that he would link up with Mao against the invaders. So, early in 1937, the two deadly enemies found themselves unexpectedly joined as allies to save the motherland.

The Japanese military responded quickly and brutally. From their base in Manchuria they drove south through eastern China, the industrial and commercial heart of the nation. Beijing and Shanghai soon fell, and by the end of 1938 most major cities, including all the ports, were in their hands.

Residents of Chongqing survey the ruins of their neighbourhood after a Japanese bombing raid. The Chinese had no answer to Japanese air superiority, and could only bitterly count the damage.

Retreat to the mountains

In face of the assault, the **Nationalist** armies fell back westward, as the Communists had done before them. Eventually Jiang established a new capital at Chongqing in Sichuan province.

But even if the Japanese controlled the cities, they had difficulty policing the countryside. Mao's Communists embarked on an energetic hit-and-run campaign, employing **guerrilla tactics** to attack isolated garrisons, supply convoys and railway lines.

Jiang's waiting game

Meanwhile, Jiang in Chongqing was biding his time. He was sure that Japan's expansionist policies would ultimately lead that nation into conflict with the western powers. In 1941 he was proved right. The Japanese launched an unprovoked attack on the American navy base at Pearl Harbor in the Pacific, and in response the USA declared war on Japan. It seemed help might be on the way at last.

THE RAPE OF NANJING

Japan's military decided to subdue the Chinese through terror. In 1937, in the **Guomindang** capital of Nanjing, the occupying forces were let loose on the civilian population. Before the eyes of horrified foreign observers, the soldiers went on a rampage of rape and killing. Subsequently an international tribunal would conclude that some 20,000 women were violated in the Rape of Nanjing and more than 200,000 men were murdered.

An unprovoked air attack on the American naval base of Pearl Harbor on 7 December 1941 brought the USA into the war against Japan. From that time on, the Chinese had a powerful ally in their struggle against the Japanese invaders.

Fight to the finish

Brief truce

The World War II years were a time of stalemate in China's own internal troubles. The Japanese held on to their gains but made few further advances; they had other things on their mind. Jiang Jieshi was playing a waiting game in Chongqing, trying to keep his armies intact to take over the country when World War II ended. The most active fighters were the **Communists**, who were still harassing the Japanese in occupied northern China.

The shaky truce between Jiang and Mao broke down early in 1941, and from then on **Nationalists** and Communists were once more at each other's throats. But that situation changed again with the Japanese surrender in August 1945. The USA and the **Soviet Union** – the two victorious powers with a direct interest in China – both had their own reasons for wanting to see the country united. So in January 1946, despite their bitter personal enmity, Mao and Jiang were once more persuaded briefly to join forces.

Longtime enemies Mao and Jiang toast each other during the brief truce, arranged with American help, in early 1946. Within three months, Communists and Nationalists were at war again, this time in a fight to the finish.

War to the bitter end

But their differences went too deep to be set aside lightly. Within three months the two sides were back at war, and there were to be no more truces.

At the time, the Nationalists seemed to have all the best cards. Their armies numbered 3.7 million men in 1945, and they had more than 1000 US-supplied planes. Against them the Communists could muster less than a tenth of that force, and only half their soldiers were armed at all.

In addition, Jiang could count on huge amounts of American aid – more than 2 billion dollars between 1945 and 1949 – while Mao received little from a Soviet Union itself weakened by war. With the Japanese withdrawal, the Nationalists also regained control of the nation's major cities and industries. Many thought that it was only a matter of time before Jiang would finally destroy the Communists and reunite the nation. But appearances were deceptive; events were to prove them terribly wrong.

Street vendors sell flags of the victorious allies to Shanghai residents celebrating the Japanese surrender at the end of World War II. The removal of the Japanese threat promised a new dawn for China, and for a time there was hope that all parties would work together to create a democratic future.

The Nationalist debacle

Corruption weakens the army

Nationalist fortunes in the **civil war** reached a high point early in 1947. For a time Jiang's forces controlled every provincial capital in China; they even managed to drive Mao from his long-established base in Yan'an. But almost at once things started to go wrong.

In fact the rot had set in earlier, in the years of enforced idleness in Sichuan. Corruption blighted the Nationalist war effort. While the officers lived well off foreign aid and taxes, the peasant soldiers often went unpaid. **Morale** was disastrously low; new recruits often had to be roped together to stop them from **deserting**. As for the Sichuanese themselves, they referred to Jiang's army as 'downriver bandits'.

The curse of inflation

At the end of World War II a new problem further undermined the Nationalist cause, and that was inflation. To pay its way, Jiang's government had printed more and more money

Red Army troops advance in the course of the crucial 1948 campaign that won them control of north-eastern China. In the fighting Jiang Jieshi lost his best troops, which were first cut off from their fellow Nationalist forces in the south and then forced to surrender.

that steadily lost its value. By 1948 the situation had spiralled out of control and prices went through the roof. In 1937 a farmer with 100 Chinese dollars could purchase two oxen, but by 1949 the same amount would buy just a sheet of paper! In 1948, the cost of rice, the nation's main food, could go up six times in a day. People's savings became worthless, and starvation stalked the streets of the cities.

With their policy of **self-sufficiency**, Mao's troops were hardly touched by the problems of inflation; they were used to living off the land and had little need for money. Now they found that Nationalist troops, paid in worthless paper, were only too willing to sell them their guns for a few handfuls of grain.

Buoyed up by the Nationalist defections, the Red Army swept across northern China, first cutting off some of Jiang's best troops in Manchuria and then disarming them. By mid-1948 they found that whole divisions were coming over to them; three-quarters of all the soldiers they captured gave up without a fight. By that autumn, the situation had been turned around. Now it was the **Communists** who had the men and the arms; the remaining Nationalists were on the run and fighting for their lives.

Looting breaks out in the streets of Nanjing in the panicky days before Communist forces moved into the city. The Nationalist capital finally fell in April 1949.

RULES OF CONDUCT

The Communist leaders imposed strict discipline over their soldiers as can be seen from this Red Army marching song.

> *Speak politely.*
> *Pay fairly for what you buy.*
> *Return everything you borrow.*
> *Pay for any damage.*
> *Don't strike or swear at people.*
> *Don't damage the crops.*
> *Don't take liberties with women.*
> *Don't mistreat captives.*

The final showdown

China 'lost' to the Communists

The outside world watched amazed as Jiang Jieshi's armies disintegrated around him. For many years afterwards, US politicians would argue over who was responsible for 'losing' China to the **Communists**. In fact the **Nationalist** forces largely self-destructed; Jiang paid the penalty for being too dependent on the cities and out of touch with the peasants who made up the bulk of China's 600 million people.

Jiang goes to Taiwan

The end came quickly. The last great battle of the **civil war** was fought from late 1948 on, around the Nationalist capital of Nanjing. The city fell in April

Red Army forces enter the old imperial capital of Beijing in January 1949. The troops were greeted as liberators and encountered no resistance.

1949, though Jiang Jieshi had already retreated, first south to Canton, then west to Sichuan where he had sought refuge from the Japanese a dozen years earlier. This time, though, he had no serious hope of regaining lost ground. Eventually he left with the remnants of his followers for the island of Formosa, now called Taiwan, in the East China Sea. There he set up the Republic of China, ruling over what he saw as a **government in exile**, ready to take control over mainland China should the political situation ever permit. His successors remain in control of Taiwan to this day.

The birth of the People's Republic

On the mainland, the victors took their time to establish control over their vast dominions. It was 1 October 1949 when Mao finally proclaimed the People's Republic of China before a crowd of a million people in Beijing's Tiananmen Square, where the advent of new dynasties had been formally proclaimed in imperial times. The note he struck in his speech was one of national pride. *'Ours will no longer be a nation subject to insult and humiliation,'* he proclaimed. *'We have stood up.'* After 22 years of civil war and invasion and more than a century of national decline, it was a message that the nation had long been waiting to hear.

The march's long shadow

Mao the social visionary

The **Communist** victory in 1949 put China in the hands of veterans of the Long March. Their exploits became part of national legend, and every Chinese schoolchild learned of heroic feats like the capture of the Luding bridge. The new rulers carried over into their system of government something of the spirit of the march itself. In power, they were as tough on corruption and greed as they had been on indiscipline and looting among the troops.

Soldiers recite from the 'little red book' containing the Thoughts of Chairman Mao. No criticism of Mao's views was permitted for, as the book itself stated, *'Not to have a correct political point of view is like having no soul'*.

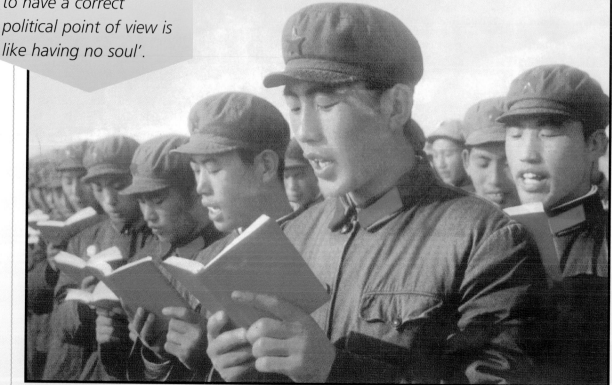

Yet there was to be no happy ending for the march's leaders themselves. Under the new government, power became increasingly concentrated in the hands of one man, Chairman Mao, a social visionary with a determination to put his ideas into practice whatever the cost. Never tolerant of criticism, Mao grew increasingly suspicious of his old comrades-in-arms, whom he came to suspect of plotting against him.

Cultural Revolution – a time of suffering

The climax came in the Cultural Revolution, a mass movement engineered by Mao in the mid-1960s to encourage what he called 'continuous revolution' in Chinese society. At its height, fanatical Red Guards fanned out across the nation in a quest to root out the 'Four Olds' – old culture, old ideas, old customs and old habits. Politically, their main targets were the very leaders who had marched and fought with Mao so long ago. Some were driven from office, others publicly humiliated or even killed.

Red Guards force suspected political opponents to wear dunce's caps in Beijing during the Cultural Revolution of the late 1960s. Those considered guilty of not following the Maoist party line were subjected to physical violence as well as public humiliation. It was later estimated that about 35,000 died as a result.

Mao's successor

Yet one did survive. Deng Xiaoping had a relatively minor role in the march itself, but later rose high in the Communist hierarchy. His family was physically attacked in the Cultural Revolution – a son was left paralyzed from the waist down – and he himself was sent to work in a tractor factory. But he managed to win his way back into favour, and when Mao finally died in 1976, it was he who won the power struggle to succeed him.

Deng remained in charge until his own death in 1997, at the ripe old age of 93. So even six decades after it finished, the Long March continued to cast its shadow over Chinese life, providing the nation's leadership up to the threshold of the new millennium.

Time-line

1912	Last emperor abdicates. End of imperial rule.
1916	Start of warlord era
1924	Nationalist Guomindang party admits Communists as members
1925	Death of Sun Zhongshan, the 'father of the Chinese Revolution'
1926	Jiang Jieshi launches Northern Expedition against warlords
1927	Jiang launches Shanghai Purge of Communists
1928	Guomindang forces capture Beijing from warlords
1930	Jiang's First Annihilation Campaign against Communists
1931	Japanese forces occupy Manchuria
1933	Fifth Annihilation Campaign launched
1934	16 October – Long March begins
1935	8 January – Mao elected Communist Party Chairman at Zunyi
	25 May – Luding suspension bridge over Dadu River captured
	October – Long March ends in Shaanxi province
1936	January – Communists set up capital at Yan'an
	December – Warlord revolt forces Jiang into alliance with Mao
1937	Japanese forces invade southern China. Rape of Nanjing.
1938	Jiang retreats from Japanese, westwards to Sichuan
1941	January – Nationalists and Communists break their truce
	7 December – Japanese attack Pearl Harbor. USA declares war.
1945	World War II ends. Japan, defeated, withdraws from China.
1946	Full-scale civil war resumes between Nationalists and Communists
1946	19 March – Nationalists capture Communist capital of Yan'an
	December – Nationalist forces defeated in Manchuria
1948	Hyper-inflation undermines Nationalist war effort
1949	21 January – Beijing falls to Communists
	1 October – Mao proclaims the People's Republic of China
	December – Nationalists complete withdrawal to Formosa (now called Taiwan)
1950	October – China invades Tibet
	November – Chinese forces intervene in Korean War
1966	Mao inaugurates the Cultural Revolution
1976	Death of Chairman Mao. Deng Xiaoping succeeds him as leader.
1997	Death of Deng Xiaoping

Glossary

abdicate	to give up power or step down from the throne
anarchy	state of lawlessness with no established order
annihilation	total destruction
civil war	war between different groups within the same country
Communist	member of a political movement dedicated to creating a society in which possessions are held in common
concubine	a secondary wife in societies where more than one is allowed
constitutional	government in keeping with an established legal framework
desertion	the wilful abandoning of a military post
dowager	a wealthy widow
enclave	a district surrounded by foreign or hostile territory
government in exile	a ruling body, forced from its native land, that hopes one day to return
guerrilla tactics	method of warfare usually involving harassment and sabotage
Guomindang	the Chinese Nationalist party set up by Sun Zhongshan
hygiene	the principles of cleanliness and good sanitation to improve health
illiterate	unable to read or write
incursion	a raid into hostile territory
indoctrination	thought control; forcible education in ideas that may not be criticized
interrogate	to question closely, often under threat of force
Marxist	reflecting the views of Karl Marx, founder of the international Communist movement
mobilize	to prepare an army for action
morale	the good feeling that a group of people has about itself
Nationalist	In China, a follower of the republican movement led first by Sun Zhongshan and then by Jiang Jieshi
private enterprise	companies owned and operated by individuals and not by the state
propaganda	misleading information meant to persuade people to adopt a certain viewpoint
puppet ruler	a ruler in name only, manipulated by others
reconnaissance	watching the enemy to discover their position and the condition of their troops
sabotaged	secretly destroyed buildings and machinery
scorched-earth	the wartime policy of destroying anything that may be useful to the enemy
self-sufficiency	a lifestyle allowing people to support themselves without the help of others
Soviet Union	a huge Communist country, including Russia, that broke up in the 1990s into separate countries
soviet	in China, an area governed along Communist lines
warlord	a ruler kept in power by military strength alone

Index